INTRODUCTION

For this, the ninth book in the *"Around"* series I have moved to the southern fringes of the B followed the A37 from Whitchurch to Clutton centred on and around Pensford. The book has been specially assembled from old photographs to enable the reader to pictorially take a nostalgic journey through the various hamlets, villages and larger communities, and the pictures chosen will hopefully stir those distant or not so distant memories, or for the younger generation simply show a glimpse of how life once was during the early years of the last century. In preparing the book it has been designed to link with the neighbouring area covered by my book *Around Keynsham*, and it is hoped that in due course others will be written to fill in any gaps and to generally expand into the surrounding area.

Over the last forty years or so Whitchurch has grown from a small village on the outskirts of Bristol, into a large dormitory area that houses the vast number of commuters that travel daily in and out of the nearby cities, but nevertheless the nucleus of the original village is still discernable, and hopefully this will be helped by the pictures contained within this book. Pensford, which is in the parish of Publow, is an old market town based around a convenient place to cross the River Chew, a waterway that has had many influences, both good and bad, upon the town and the surrounding district. With a settlement growing around the crossing place, the community grew as the river was harnessed and used to operate a number of woollen cloth mills, from the ready supply of raw material scattered around the nearby hills and vales. The river itself was diverted into a number of mill-channels, and this may have contributed to the high level of flooding that has taken place, bringing with it its own destruction, particularly on the night of 10/11th July 1968, when up to seven feet of water smashed through part of the village destroying both properties and the original turnpike bridge. Before the Bristol Turnpike Trust constructed, during the nineteenth century, a new road, travellers on their way through the village to Bristol would have to come along what is now known as Pensford Old Road, into the High Street, turn right opposite the village lock-up, into Church Street, over the river, and then out of the village up Pensford Hill. When it was constructed the turnpike cut a swathe through the community, with a new road, and a new bridge, which almost isolated the two halves of the existing town. The manufacture of woollen cloth declined as new materials became available, and wool lost its dominance, causing new employment and new finance to be needed if the area was to survive, and gradually the importance of coal began to dominate the village, firstly with mines being dug in the surrounding area, notably in Clutton, then with the demand to construct a railway to bring the coal from the mines to the customers, involving the need to construct the magnificent railway viaduct that has towered over the village for the past 130 years or so; as for Pensford itself, the first pit was sunk during 1909, and worked continuously for the next fifty years. To the east of Pensford the River Chew flows towards Publow and then onto Keynsham where it joins the River Avon, whereas to the south the turnpike road takes the traveller to Chelwood and Clutton, with both places being featured in this book, and on the inside back cover.

In its production I am grateful to Mike Tozer, and Janet and Derek Fisher, and others who have allowed me to include pictures from their individual collections, and to Sheila Brooks for reading through the transcript, and those residents of Clutton who kindly assisted me with my research. At all times I have endeavoured to minimize any mistakes made but should any exist then they are unfortunately of my own making, for which I apologize and trust that any such errors will not distract you from enjoying the remaining contents.

May 2006   Ian S Bishop

"It's a nice day for a trip into the countryside or we might even get as far as Weston-s-Mare." Obviously an organised outing and a posed photograph with, the first three vehicles all Bristol built 4 ton 28 seat charabancs, FB2617 borrowed from the Bath Bus Company, followed by HT1511 and HT1512 from Bristol Tramways Co. Note all the vehicles are running on solid tyres, without a great deal of scope for much comfort, but almost certainly everyone on board thoroughly enjoyed the novel experience of having a days outing, c1923.

With the camera turned around and looking back towards Bristol, a neat and tidy school boy, with regulatory shorts and cap happily stands in the middle of Wells Road, something unlikely to be recommended today. With what appears to be a building site on the left, the junction with Maggs Lane can just be seen behind the large telegraph pole, whilst opposite is the frontage of the United Reform Church c1935. How peaceful Whitchurch must have seemed in those days, with little or no traffic, and little or no clutter of street furniture, although of course they did have the inconvenience of having no pavement along one side of the road.

The Village. Whitchurch, Nr. Bristol.

Looking towards the hub of the village on a sunny morning. A group of residents mull over the events of the day, whilst a gentleman, with a smart straw boater, keeps an eye on the photographer, as does another local who is casually standing in the road in the full knowledge that it was perfectly safe to do so, after all neither the horse nor the dog are going anywhere. Church Road is off to the right; the future hustle and bustle is at least half a century away, the Great War is over and the scars are beginning to heal c1922.

In this view of the centre of Whitchurch the photographer has taken his camera past the Church Road junction ~ seen on the left ~ and has captured an historical scene of the village as it once was, with Staunton Lane off to the right, the main building in this picture has been replaced by the present site of the Maes Knoll Inn. Note the village pump on the right and the man with his straw boater determined to be in the picture, c1920.

Staunton Lane looking towards Stockwood, although when this picture was taken very little if anything other than fields existed in Stockwood. The cameraman, in this circa 1910 view has certainly aroused the curiosity of the locals who have decided that they would like to have their photograph taken without of course realising they were about to be frozen in time, nor did they realise that they were producing such an evocative community scene and dress that would soon be lost for ever.

Was this the original corner shop for the village of Whitchurch, situated as it is at the junction of Church Road and Bristol Road, and aptly named *The Supply*. The photographer has grouped together as many of the villagers as possible, and it being a working day, apparently only the ladies and the children were available, to be frozen in time and to give us just a glimpse of this segment of village life around the early 1920's.

Back along the main Bristol Road with the branches of the same tree as in the previous picture still offering its shade, and the start of the motorised traffic that one-day will plague the village and the surrounding area. In this circa 1930 picture there are just three vehicles parked without any restrictions near the newly evolving garage. Apart from these new intruders, almost certainly seen by their owners as a wonderful invention, Whitchurch at this time, has still retained its peaceful air of tranquillity.

The railway first went through Whitchurch during the late 1850's, but with problems besetting the "Bristol & North Somerset Railway", it was not until September 1873 that the first passenger train passed through the village, and even then there was nowhere for it to stop as the halt did not open until 1st January 1925. What a wonderful asset this little halt would have been with today's level of traffic congestion if only someone had had the foresight to retain the line and the passenger access for commuter services. Picture c 1930

A very tranquil and rural scene without a building in sight, just the wonderings of Rookery Lane, Norton Malreward, but if legend is to be believed this was once the site of enormous strength and brutality. It has been said that at nearby Norton Hawkfield there once lived a giant of a man who was not averse to showing off his strength and to impress his king, who happened to be visiting the area, the giant picked up three of the king's soldiers, and bodily carried them up the tower of the parish church. The soldiers unhappy with their treatment struggled to get

Rookery Lane,
Norton Malreward, Somt.

away, which made the giant ~ Sir John Hautville angry, and holding the men more tightly, crushed the life out of each soldier. Unconcerned by the loss of three soldiers, Edward l was so impressed that he gave Sir John the parish land. On his part Sir John considered that his efforts deserved far more than the small amount of parish land and that the king's reward was poor or a "mal" reward for his efforts.

On the right the River Chew tumbles along its meanderings somewhere between Stanton Court and Pensford c 1935

The Stones, Stanton Drew.

The name Stanton means "the place of the stones," and in these two pictures it is very understandable why the area was given that name, with Drew being the thirteenth century family who held the manor. A number of legends have grown up around the stones and their origin, but the one thing that is certain is that they have nothing whatsoever to do with Druids. In total there are three stone circles, plus a cove and an avenue that leads down to the river and connects the Great and the Northeastern circles. The purpose and origin of the stone circles/avenue is uncertain, but it is believed that the stones were brought to the area and erected during the Neolithic period between 2000 and 1400 BC possibly as a ritual site to make offerings for the dead.

As for one of the more attractive legends, it is said that the Cove and circles represent a wedding party that were punished for marrying and dancing on a Sunday, by being petrified. The Cove is said to represent the parson and the bride and groom, whilst the large circle represents the guests, and the small circle depicts the accompanying musicians. With a diameter of around 345 feet, the Stanton Drew circle or henge is the second largest stone circle in the country. Both pictures are c1920

Druid Stones - Stanton Drew

ROUND HOUSE   STANTON DREW

Two slightly different angled views of the fifteenth century, thatched roof round house built on the small-grassed triangle at the head of *"Old Tarnwell"* at its junction with Pensford Lane. On the left is a picture taken on a bright warm summer's day with two small children watching the photographer with great interest, having themselves recently emerged from the front door of the building, whilst in the background a cyclist makes

Toll House, Stanton Drew.

18013.

steady progress towards Pensford. Note the shutter swung back from the downstairs window, with a sign above directing the traveller to Stanton Drew and Stanton Wick c1922. When, during the eighteenth century, Pensford Lane was taken over by the Bristol Turnpike Trust the house was acquired and changed to a Toll House as seen by the picture on the right c1931.

It was probably an extremely unusual event in these children's lives to see a man with a large tripod camera taking pictures, and no doubt with his encouragement, and their natural curiosity it did not take very long to pose the eighteen children across the muddy road. In the grounds of the Post Office on the right, there are two bashful adults who are almost incidental to the composition of the picture. Note the cheeky grin and casual stance of the boy on the left in total contrast to the facial expression of the girl in the dark dress just a few feet away, c1908.

The caption on the right-hand card reads *"Mrs Hinge's Tea Gardens,"* but apart from a group of children in fancy dress, custom would on this day seem somewhat sparse with plenty of empty chairs and tables. Regrettably, the exact location of these tea gardens has not yet been achieved nor has the identification of the children can anyone help? c 1906.

The large and extensive vicarage at Stanton Drew complete with its own half-size lean-to glasshouse, did the vicar have time on his hands for the necessary cultivation, or was the church able to support the expense of one or two gardeners. Picture taken from a card written by the vicar's wife, a Mrs Williams, and posted in Pensford on the 25th July 1907.

Slanton Drew

In the bright winter sunlight Bromley Road just past its junction with Sandy lane is seen looking towards Stanton Court, with a group of village lads studying the antics of the photographer, c1902

14

The caption clearly states Victoria Cottage, Stanton Drew and shows its rustic nature with the carter and his children posed beside the means of scraping together a living, however the exact location of the picture has eluded me. Taken from a card posted around 1904, the sender identifies the carter as Fred ———— out with *Doss*

On the right is a view of the eight hundred year old church of St Mary the Virgin. Like many churches built during the thirteenth and fourteenth centuries, our Victorian ancestors had their own ideas of restoration, and much of the present interior was reconstructed one hundred and fifty years ago. The bowl of the font situated in the north aisle dates back to the Norman period of our history. Picture c 1908

PENSFORD

Looking down Pensford Hill from close to its junction with Station Approach at a time when motor vehicles were still few and far between; the left-hand villas are bathed in bright sunlight with just two persons strolling down the hill. Note the sign for Henley Tyres, c1950.

Further down Pensford Hill and further back in time. Here we see a moustached gentleman standing outside of *"Rose Bank"* house, whilst his dog sits patiently on the pavement but is ready to spring into action should the pony decide to awake from its repose. Behind a carter exchanges a word or two with the family standing outside their cottage, and like the nearest pony, the rest of Pensford slumbers c1925.

Despite the misleading title this is a very similar view to the one above but it is a picture that takes us even further back in time to around 1904. It could be the local Postman leaning on the fence with his dog at his side, whilst opposite a baker delivers his products. Church Road and the *"Rising Sun"* can be clearly seen in the background

STATION ROAD, PENSFORD. 469.

PENSFORD

The sun shines brightly on a peaceful corner of Pensford prior to the onslaught of cars and lorries that would profoundly change the village forever, although the preparations have started with the installation of the cat's-eyes in the middle of Pensford Hill. Just one car ~ OY9604 is in view, the Post office is on the right, the lady looks towards the only other person in the picture as he strolls down Church Street towards the *Rising Sun* an old eighteenth coaching inn, whilst the top of the church tower can be seen above the rooftops c 1950.

Where Pensford Hill meets Church Street at a time when it was perfectly safe for the photographer to arrange to have fourteen children, including one in a homemade pram, to be spread-eagled, across the main road and have their photograph taken. On the right is a small group of children who need that extra bit of coaxing from the adults before they get in the picture. The ivy covered building on the left, with the lady standing outside is now the home of the village Post Office. The house on the extreme right no longer exists, c1908.

A general panorama of Pensford looking down across the area where Pensford Hill joins New Road at its junction with Church Street. Although the River Chew is hidden from view, a bridge incorporated in New Road crosses it at this point and during the July 1968 night of the Great Flood, the deluge washed a substantial section of that bridge away, c 1955.

In this view, taken from the railway viaduct, the sweep of New Road can be seen at a slightly different angle, whilst to the right the church of St Thomas a Beckett stands above the properties that cluster around Church Street, c 1908

Main Street Pensford

New Street, with the impressive backdrop of the railway viaduct dwarfing all of the houses, is seen as HHY 598, a Bristol double-decker bus with a low bridge body, negotiates itself around the only two cars appearing in the picture that happen to be both inconveniently parked on the bend at the bottom of a steep hill, enters the village before preparing itself for a possible exchange of passengers, before proceeding on its way to Wells. Note the railway signal on the viaduct, the country style painted telephone box, and the old bridge across the River Chew, c 1948.

PENSFORD

By today's standards, this is a view of a very quiet New Road from a slightly different angle showing, on the right, more of the village school. The bus, which is on route 137 to Shepton Mallet, is picking up fresh passengers, whilst a gentleman in jodhpurs watches on, and across the road is a group of people no doubt waiting the arrival of a bus to take them into Bristol. The high density and pace of traffic is yet to come as this c 1950 snapshot encapsulates a view of life in Pensford as it once was.

The parish church of St. Thomas a Beckett stands on its own island caused by the manmade creation of the mill leat and the natural flow of the River Chew. When the devastating floods of July 1968 hit the village the rushing water swept over the island and through the church and caused irreparable damage from which the building has never fully recovered, picture c1955.

Pensford Church & River.

PSD.18 THE CHURCH, PENSFORD

In the early afternoon of a bright summers day, a cameraman leaned over the left-hand parapet of the nineteenth century river bridge to allow him to take a more panoramic view of St Thomas a Beckett, and of an exceedingly quiet traffic free Church Street, c 1955. The floods of July 1968 caused so much havoc to the fabric of the church that since that date the building has remained unused.

A very peaceful and sleepy Church Street taken from the old bridge, with just one young lady in her "Sunday best" to animate the picture. On the right is a small shop owned by Mrs Rachel Hazell, advertising Fry's Chocolates, whilst in the background is the *"Rising Sun"* next to another village shop at Mill Corner; during the night of the 10/11 July 1968 a wall of flood water over six feet high swept through this tranquil scene. Dominating the picture with its height and majesty is part of the railway viaduct, c 1910.

A much more animated view of Church Street with the village children determined to get into the picture. The young lad in the foreground leans nonchalantly against the parapet, others stand and wait not quite sure what is about to happen, whilst on the right, the goodies in Mrs Hazell's shop window hold a great deal of appeal for one young man if not for his companions, c 1922.

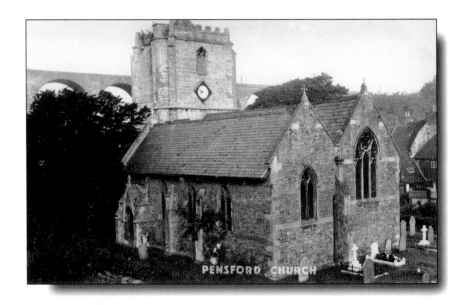

Whilst the top right-hand picture shows the south side of the church around 1950, the reflection of the church tower and the general view are both around fifty years older. The body of the church was completely rebuilt during 1868, only the tower is original. Although it is not clear, the railway station and goods yards with a rake of trucks can just be seen in the general view. Note the artificial clouds drawn to enhance the picture.

CHURCH ST. PENSFORD

With the camera moved on and turned ninety degrees, we can now look back down Church Street with the *Rising Sun* on the right, and *Nelson House* on the left. Children can run happily along the street, as it is no longer part of the main coaching road through the village from Wells to Bristol, even a small child on her own is not in danger as such was life in this small but historically important corner of Pensford, c 1950

Modern Pensford would somehow not be quite the same without having its established and famous railway viaduct as a backcloth. On the right the photographer has gone out of the village along Stanton Lane and looked back and framed the church with one of the sixteen arches, and allowed glimpses of the village through other arches, c 1955

The Viaduct,
Pensford.

Twelve of the sixteen arches are captured in this view, and it will be seen that due to the topography of the valley floor they are not all symmetrical. Built during the 1860's, to carry the North Somerset Railway and opened to passenger services in 1873, the viaduct is just under one thousand feet long, and stands around 95 feet above the river, which was to become its nemesis as it was decided that the 1968 floods had damaged the structure to make it unsafe, and the railway was closed, which was of course, what the railway authorities wanted in the first place, c 1902

The grandeur and craftsmanship of the Victorian workman can be clearly seen in the picture on the left as the viaduct sweeps across the Chew valley and dwarfs little Pensford below. This picture, which has been reproduced by kind permission of R E Toop, was taken on the 2nd May 1959 when the railway was still fully operational. In the background Pensford Goods Shed and station can be seen

Hauled by an ex Great Western 2-6-2T prairie tank engine sporting its new British Railway livery a two coach stopping train hurries away from Pensford Station and crosses the viaduct during the evening sunshine on its journey from Bristol [TM]] to Frome, c1956. Regrettably, when this picture was taken the idea of commuting by train was held by only a very small minority, as most of us aspired to owning and using our own car to travel to and from work; if only the clock could be put back.

Taken at almost the same spot is another Bristol [TM] to Frome two coach stopping train, with this time the 2-6-2T-prairie tank engine, 5542 running bunker first. Taken on the 2nd May 1959, this picture has also been reproduced by kind permission of R E Toop.

The neat and well-appointed station at Pensford created a crossing point for trains going in opposite directions to pass each other. The station consisted of an up and down line platform, although the down line platform was devoid of any buildings. Although only a handful of passenger trains passed through each day the staff maintained a clean and tidy station as can clearly be seen in this photograph taken around 1958.

Above: although the down line platform has been taken out of commission, following the removal of the track, there is still the need for the signalman to hand over to the driver the token to allow the train to enter the next section. Here the fireman of an unidentified 2-6-2T engine can be seen handing over his token whilst the signalman ~ the signal box can be seen on the left~ is ready to provide the next token, c 1959. The small picture on the right shows the position of the signal box on the platform in relation to the other station buildings, all of which are now beginning to show their age, c 1961

On the left is a view of the River Chew as it flows over the weir with, in the background, two of the massive columns built to create the arch to carry the railway across the valley some ninety-five feet above the river. The sender of the card considered that this little bit of Pensford "is prettier than Porlock Weir," c 1910.

The two lower pictures are described as "The old Mill Stream and demonstrate how the power of the river was harnessed and show what this part of Pensford looked like around 1904.

Having now moved across the New Road and entered High Street, one of the first buildings we come across is the original Post Office, as seen on the right, with the postmistress standing in the doorway, with assistant and the family cat. According to the sign on the wall, you can obtain Money Orders, use it as a Savings Bank, send parcels and telegraphs, purchase Insurance Annuities, and partake in the Express Delivery Business. Note the Newbury Furniture sign higher on the wall advertising its Queen Street, Bristol premises, and the letterbox incorporated in the window, c1905.

Below is a sample of when Pensford had its own rubber-franking stamp to cancel the postage paid.

Pensford Post Office.

Ye Olde Street, Pensford

Although described on the picture as *"Ye Olde Street"* it is officially known as High Street, with the view looking up towards its junction with Publow Lane and Pensford Old Road. Behind the young lad, who is doing his bit to keep the street clean despite wearing his best clothes, is the eighteenth century octagonal lock up, where any criminal and/or drunk could be incarcerated overnight in the hope that he might have cooled-of by the morning. At this time the proprietor of the grocer's shop was William Chivers, c 1902

Pensford

Season's Greetings

With this seasonal greetings card we have an opportunity of seeing most of Pensford at a moment when more than one hundred years ago it was frozen in time by an unknown photographer. In the background is the railway embankment leading from the Station past the signal box and the Goods Shed and onto the viaduct, with a number of empty trucks waiting their turn to take Pensford's coal around the country. Some of the larger buildings including the Wesleyan Methodist chapel can be clearly seen, as can the old river bridge destroyed in the floods of 1968, whilst in the centre of the picture is the Pensford Council school built in 1898 to accommodate 170 children. At the time of the picture Mr Alfred Hayes was the Head teacher, c 1902.

This was once the main road through the village either to or from Bristol to Wells, and the *George and Dragon* on the left played an important part as the staging post for horse-drawn coaches from at least 1752, and the tall entrance shows where the coach would be taken and for fresh horses to be harnessed whilst, no doubt, the occupants of the coach refreshed themselves in the inn. In the background is a horse-drawn coach whilst in addition to two young ladies and four children, the photographer has also asked the local postman to stop and have his picture taken, c 1903.

PENSFORD

014

This shows an overall view of the village from a slightly different angle to the one seen on the seasonal greetings card reproduced on page 35. Not only was this photograph taken during the summer months, it was also taken some five years after the earlier picture; however during that time little has changed to sleepy old Pensford as the buildings bathe in the warm sunshine, and the only person abroad is a man with horse and cart who is about to plod his way into Church Street, c 1908

PENSFORD
NEW COLLIERY

This was once a very familiar sight in Pensford when the extraction and distribution of coal was probably the most important source of employment in the area before its demise during the late 1950's. It is difficult to be exactly certain what is happening in this posed picture, bricks are being brought by wheelbarrow from one part of the pithead to another to be stacked for future use. Only the two on the left give the impression of being underground workers, the rest would all appear to be surface/maintenance workers, c 1910

In this picture the camera has been moved to the left, and not only shows the bulk of the winding gear but also part of the internal railway system, and a row of boilers on the left; once again the photographer has posed the men, which slightly stifles the overall picture, c1908

The fifteenth century "Somerset style" tower of All Saints Church stands as a proud sentinel over the medieval stone bridge and the flowing Chew that in years gone by provided the main power that in turn produced the wealth and the employment in what was once an industrial parish. During the eighteenth century and no doubt even earlier there was at least one grist mill in the village, which was subsequently converted into a tin-plate mill, and which by 1780 had been acquired by Elton & Tyndall for the rolling and hammering of copper, c1910

The Sumachs   Publow. Pensford

Publow Church & River

Three further views of Publow all taken around 1903/04. As charming as the river now is it was once, during the eighteenth/nineteenth centuries, used as the vehicle to carry away the effluence produced by the local tanning industry. In the hot summer months, Publow had its own rather distinctive bouquet that helped put money into the pockets of the local Brodribbe family.

A trilogy of Queen Charlton with two separate views of the "village green." On the left a gentleman is about to climb onto his bicycle and head towards Keynsham, with an attractive thatched roof cottage behind, whilst below the tower of St Margaret's dominates the centre of the village. Almost certainly the first part of the village name is due to the fact that Catherine Parr ~ the last wife of Henry Vlll ~ held the Manor of Charlton. Below left is the view of the eighteenth-century facade and formal gardens of the Manor House, however there are many seventeenth century artefacts.

CHELWOOD RECTORY. N? BRISTOL.

This picture of Chelwood could almost be regarded as the geographical centre of the village, and was taken at a time when it was perfectly safe to stand in the middle of the road, without a care in the world and have your photograph taken. Behind the smartly dressed lady and partially hidden by the trees stands the Rectory. Note the overgrown hedge on the right, and the narrowness of the A368, and although taken around 1912 it is still a very recognizable view today.

This is the reverse but even older view of the same cottages as seen on page 43 and before the narrow door in the front wall had been blocked in. Taken from a card posted in August 1909 and written from Chelwood Rectory, the author, possibly the vicar's wife states, *these houses are next door to the Rectory.* Coal was mined in Chelwood until well into the eighteenth-century, and these properties may once have been miner's cottages. Picture c1905

New Post Office Corner, Chelwood   No. 3789

The main A368 road draws a large S shape as it sweeps through the heart of this peaceful village, and when this moment in time was frozen for us forever, the almost continuous and dense volume of traffic had not yet materialized, and with less cars, there is still time for the locality to support a village Post Office and a general store, c 1958

Malt House Farm, Chelwood   No. 3624

Approaching Chelwood from the west, with Malt House Farm on the right c 1958.

Looking back towards Post Office corner, with the business now offering petrol for sale, c 1958

Chelwood   No. 3622

The original Post Office was housed along a muddy track in an old outhouse, attached to what appears to be a thatched roof farm house in a very rural setting, c1903

A brief photo halt as one of the Bath Electric Tramways double deck buses [a Milnes Daimler, with Christopher Dodson body] takes a happy group of Edwardians on an exhilarating excursion to either Burrington Coombe or Cheddar Gorge. It looks as though the majority of passengers have gone onto the top deck for the purpose of being in this staged photograph; the ladies are all wearing fancy bonnets, and the men are bowler-hatted. With over hanging trees unlikely to have been cut to allow for the height of the bus, only the hardy would stay on top when the bus continued on its journey, c 1907

Chelwood House looking somewhat bleak and foreboding in its thick covering of ivy, in great contrast to the bright image it portrays today. Built in 1681 as the Dower House for the Cecil family the house faces onto the main A37, and is surrounded by almost one and a half acres of land, mostly turned over to formal gardens. Taken from a card used for Christmas/New Year Greetings c1905

Taken when the Upper Bristol Road was little more than a rural country lane with a pair of isolated cottages built on "The Flat" in the eighteenth century, which are now known as *Kimberly* and *Tumbleweed*. Probably built as miner's cottages they were once part of the Warwick Estate and today are part of a small cluster of distinct properties that help give Clutton its three integral sections, c1904

THE FLAT, CLUTTON.

Bristol Road, Clutton.

The Upper Bristol Road looking from Temple Cloud towards Bristol. On the left is *The Old Manse* and behind the dominating tree the end on view of the *Warwick Arm* can be seen, whilst on the right is *Forge House;* ~ the blacksmith's forge is just out of shot on the extreme right of the picture; next comes *Ingeldene* and *Plum Tree Cottage,* all names of the present century but not necessarily in existence when the picture was taken around 1908. Note the complete absence of any traffic, and the stylised clouds, also to be seen in the general view of Pensford picture on page 26.

Looking along Station Road with the start of Broomhill Lane just visible on the left, Church Lane on the right. Both the Methodists Chapel and the Independents Chapel can be seen in the bright sunlight on the left, whilst further down the road is the free school building, as part of Clutton has been frozen in time and can be seen by us as it was over one hundred years ago, c1905

The title given to the view on the right is "Jacobs Bottom ~ Clutton," a description not likely to be found on any modern day map, but the building in the foreground is easily identified as *"Burchell House"* whilst the one in the distance is almost certainly the *"Cross Keys."* This is the Old Bristol Road taken from close to the present day junction with Maypole Close, whilst Burchill Close would be on the right, c1905.

A very rural and old scene of the Bendalls Bridge area of Clutton where so much has changed over the years, although the "lean-to" in the foreground still exists. Beyond, the eighteenth century reddish sandstone tower of St Augustine's church can be seen peaking out from behind the dominating tree whilst beneath the same tree there are two little girls strolling along the dusty track that acts as the road and who are just about to pass the cottages subsequently pulled down in the mid 1930's and replaced by more hygienic properties with electricity and running water, c 1908.

Looking up Station Road towards the front of *The Railway Inn* at a time before it expanded into the size it is today. Behind the photographer, the road went under a bridge that carried the railway line away from the village station and on towards Temple Cloud and Hallatrow c1904

Now officially known as Cook's Hill Station Road, here we have a 1905 view of Jessie Cook's Hill looking towards Station Road and the other third section of the village based around the Primary School, and the village Pub.

Jessie Cook's Hill. Clutton.

Collinson. C.S. & Co. B.

Clutton Post Office.

With nearly all of the properties shown in this picture no longer in existence it is difficult to place its exact location however, with the wall on the left still protecting the Primary School and beyond the light shaded building extant it is possible to identify this picture as being a hundred year old snapshot of Station Road, with the village postman posed outside of the first village Post Office, and the delivery van and driver patiently waiting in the background for the photographer to capture an image no longer available to us, c 1905

Two separate views of the Gaston Avenue trees, whilst on the left a large group from the Baptist Itinerant Society have, on the 17th May 1910, gathered on the primary school playground to have their picture taken, almost certainly the majority of those in the group did not come from Clutton, but had probably travelled from all over the South West and beyond.

In order to tap into the bulk movement of coal from the important Somerset Coalfields, the Bristol & North Somerset Railway was constructed in the early 1870's to link with the Wiltshire, Somerset and Weymouth Railway, but with the additional passenger revenue in mind they also built a station at Clutton together with the doubling of the track so that trains in opposite directions could pass each other. Opened on the 3rd September 1873, the B&NSR remained independent, but needed to use GWR rolling stock/motive power, becoming fully absorbed by that company in July 1884. This picture was taken around 1958, some nine years before the complete closure of the line in 1967.

The Upper Bristol Road looking in the opposite direction to the view seen on page 48 with *Plum Tree Cottage; Ingeldene and Forge House* now on the left. The darker building partially hidden by the bushes is the village forge and beyond, the tall property is situated on the corner of Jessie Cook's Hill. Most of the buildings on the left still remain whilst those on the right have made way for road improvements, but it would hardly be safe for a little girl and cart to stand in the same position today, c1910.

Bendalls Bridge looking towards Church Square and the houses that once stood in front of St Augustine, all pulled down to make room for a rural car park that more often than not is empty. The large building on the right was originally the home of a Mr Elm, but subsequently was used as a village hall/scout hall. As for Mr Elm he completely rebuilt the adjoining cottages before moving into them. None of the cottages on display had running water, having instead to rely upon an outside standpipe. Note the old lady amongst the brambles on the right, c1910.

On the right in its early days is Clutton Primary School, Station Road. Taken from a card postally used on the 5th February 1906, the sender acknowledges receipt of a very nice post card and says that they will send some better ones later on, adding that this card is not up to much! Fortunately for us the card was sent and retained and allows us a small insight of the school building as it appeared over one hundred years ago.

However Clutton is viewed it is difficult to pinpoint what might be regarded as a village centre, instead the district is favoured with three separate communities one of which is based around St Augustine's church as seen on the left. Although the reddish sandstone tower dates from the seventeen hundreds, much of the remaining body of the church was restored during the Victorian period, c1905

Forming another of the three sections of Clutton is that part of the village that huddles around the main Upper Bristol Road as seen in this picture, which shows a lone motorcyclist heading towards Temple Cloud, whilst passing, on the right, the local hostelry known as *The Warwick Arms*. Also in the picture and coming up the hill towards the photographer is an old style Ford Popular on its way to Pensford and beyond, and further study shows that before the hustle and bustle of modern day traffic levels, there is just one other vehicle in sight on what is an otherwise deserted road, c1962, how things have changed in a little over forty years!

Not only has the camera been moved down the hill and turned around from the previous picture, it has also been moved back in time by around fifty years, as we now look at a close up of *The Warwick Arms,* which was built as a Coaching Inn during the 1700's. The photographer has obviously asked the current landlord, staff and a customer to stand under the portico and a local carter to stand his horse, to help make what might have been a dull picture more interesting, c 1911

With a curious cat prepared to have a closer look at the cameraman, other residents of Jessie Cook's Hill prefer to hang back and not get too close just in case the photographer takes more than their picture. Encapsulating forever a small section of village life, as it was around 1912, the cottage on the right is now more familiarly known as No. 86 Cooks Hill, Station Road. On the left the grass in the field has been cut ready for haymaking.

The junction of the Old Bristol Road coming in from the left, with Station Road around 1911. Has the photographer persuaded one or two of the village folk to stand outside their cottages to have their picture taken, or are they there to see what the local tinker has brought on his cart. The ivy covered private house in the centre of this view has now become *"The Railway Inn"*, whilst the cottages on the left no longer exsist.

Amongst the young and not so young ladies of Clutton there is great excitement as dressed in their best, the members of the *Girls' Friendly Society* pose for the photographer in the comfort of the horse-drawn passenger wagons, in anticipation of their intended Outing to Bath, and the many shops to be found in that fair City. The Old Bristol Road at its junction with Station Road, June 1912.

The unmade road of Venus Lane looking towards the church when this part of Clutton was a very parochial and rural area, although not so far away was the industrial and difficult activity of extracting coal from the ground. It is believed that the little girl was Lilly Tavener and that the picture was taken around 1908. With trees hiding the church and modern residential infilling it is difficult to recognize the view as it was.